Devotions

PHOENIX POETS

BRUCE SMITH

Devotions

THE UNIVERSITY OF CHICAGO PRESS
Chicago & London

BRUCE SMITH teaches at Syracuse University and is the author of five books of poems, most recently of *Songs for Two Voices* (2005) and *The Other Lover* (2000), which was a finalist for both the National Book Award and the Pulitzer Prize.

The University of Chicago Press, Chicago 60637
The University of Chicago Press, Ltd., London
© 2011 by The University of Chicago
All rights reserved. Published 2011
Printed in the United States of America
20 19 18 17 16 15 14 13 12 11   2 3 4 5

ISBN-13: 978-0-226-76435-1 (paper)
ISBN-10: 0-226-76435-4 (paper)

Library of Congress Cataloging-in-Publication Data
Smith, Bruce, 1946–
    Devotions / Bruce Smith.
        p. cm. — (Phoenix poets series)
    ISBN-13: 978-0-226-76435-1 (pbk. : alk. paper)
    ISBN-10: 0-226-76435-4 (pbk. : alk. paper)
    I. Title. II. Series: Phoenix poets.
    PS3569.M512D48 2011
    811'.54—dc22   2010027119

♾ The paper used in this publication meets the minimum requirements of the American National Standard for Information Sciences—Permanence of Paper for Printed Library Materials, ANSI Z39.48-1992.

CONTENTS

Acknowledgments ix

Devotion: Coin-Op 3
Devotion: Hörlust 4
Devotion: New York, July 6
Devotion: Thirst Reduction 7
Devotion: Redshift 8
Devotion: Smoke 10
Devotion: High School 11
Devotion: Hunan House 13
Devotion: Soup 14
Devotion: Fort Drum 16
Devotion: Medea 17
Devotion: Red Roof Inn 18
Devotion: Guitar 20
Devotion: The Burnt-Over District 21
Devotion: Dub 22
Devotion: Obbligato 24
Devotion: Rent 26
Devotion: Dizzy Gillespie 28
Devotion: J's Dream 30
Devotion: Al Green 32
Devotion: Paris 33
Devotion: Contraband 34
Devotion: New York, 1970 35
Devotion: Josephine P 37
Devotion: Changeling 39
Devotion: The Garment District 40
Devotion: *Wuthering Heights* 41
Devotion: Sleep 43

Devotion: Bus to Utica 44

Devotion: Providence 46

Devotion: Syracuse 48

Devotion: Syracuse en Rose 50

Devotion: Dress 52

Devotion: *Closer* 54

Devotion: Flight 55

Devotion: Ode 56

Devotion: October 58

Devotion: Amerika 60

Devotion: Rimbaud 61

Devotion: The Game 63

Devotion: Baseball 64

Devotion: X 65

Devotion: Infant Joy 66

Devotion: Infant Sorrow 67

Devotion: The Republic 68

Devotion: Active Shooter Protocol 69

Devotion: Car Wreck 70

Devotion: Nature 71

Devotion: The Insects 72

Devotion: Dusk 74

Devotion: Race Traitor 75

Devotion: Futurismo 77

Devotion: Sun 79

Devotion: Midrash 81

Devotion: Crows 83

Devotion: Roman 85

Devotion: The Unbidden 87

Devotion: Fly 88

ACKNOWLEDGMENTS

The author wishes to thank the editors of the following publications in which these poems, some in slightly different versions, have appeared:

Agni: "Devotion: Dub," "Devotion: Fly"

American Poetry Review: "Devotion: Soup," "Devotion: Hunan House," "Devotion: Fort Drum," "Devotion: J's Dream," "Devotion: *Closer*," "Devotion: Red Roof Inn," "Devotion: Paris"

Antioch Review: "Devotion: Guitar" (as "Devotion: Les Paul")

Caesura: "Devotion: Crows"

Cavalier: "Devotion: Active Shooter Protocol," "Devotion: The Insects," "Devotion: Nature"

Dossier: "Devotion: Midrash"

Ecotone: "Devotion: *Wuthering Heights*"

Fogged Clarity: "Devotion: Providence," "Devotion: Dress"

Free Verse: "Devotion: Dusk," "Devotion: Sun"

Gulf Coast: "Devotion: Coin-Op"

Hunger Mountain: "Devotion: Infant Joy," "Devotion: Infant Sorrow"

Kenyon Review: "Devotion: Rent"

Literary Imagination: "Devotion: Smoke"

Margie: "Devotion: Bus to Utica," "Devotion: High School"

Mary: "Devotion: Ode"

Meridian: "Devotion: Car Wreck," "Devotion: Race Traitor," "Devotion: Thirst Reduction"

New Orleans Review: "Devotion: Syracuse," "Devotion: Sleep"

The New Yorker: "Devotion: The Game"

The Paris Review: "Devotion: New York, July," "Devotion: Rimbaud"

Ploughshares: "Devotion: Al Green"

Poetry: "Devotion: Obbligato," "Devotion: Josephine P," "Devotion: The Garment District," "Devotion: The Burnt-Over District," "Devotion: Baseball"

Poetry Northwest: "Devotion: October," "Devotion: Hörlust," "Devotion: The Unbidden"

Red Mountain Review: "Devotion: New York, 1970"

Slate Magazine: "Devotion: Contraband"

Stone Canoe: "Devotion: The Republic," "Devotion: Changeling"

Tikkun: "Devotion: Futurismo"

Tin House: "Devotion: Redshift" (as "Devotion: Red Shift"), "Devotion: X," "Devotion: Medea"

Washington Square: "Devotion: Flight," "Devotion: Roman"

XConnect: "Devotion: Dizzy Gillespie"

The Yale Review: "Devotion: Syracuse en Rose"

"Devotion: Amerika" appeared in *The Best of the Prose Poem: An International Journal* (Buffalo, NY: White Pine Press, 2000)

Devotions

DEVOTION: COIN-OP

When I can't make or do anything, I can always change
some bills to silver and the costumes of my self to cloth. I can
lug my fetid stuff three blocks in a gym bag as I would a corpse
where a machine can't stomach the creases, but then wolfs a Washington
like the local reserve or the lesser luck of a slot machine that gives back
what it took—current for tender—the American, empirical, diminuendo
of my hopes for capital. On the Laundromat TV: *Abrázame Muy Fuerte*—
a soap washing the English out with stylish overlove. The Ethiopian
shirtdress tumbles with the double knit and T-shirt and flannels
of the unstylish boroughs. Swish of nun's veil and voile, the boy shorts,
boxers, briefs—the names of undergarments like the names of god,
hushed or unspoken, triumphant or cursed. On the screen the nurse/
ingénue kisses the patient/hero on the lips and it's the gamut
of ravishment, affliction, fraudulence, magnificence, anguish, or argument
for or against art. It's a wish to stop for a moment at a place ransacked
of bias or bitterness by the pixilated acts and cleaned of your stink and grease,
your self-embraces against the ticks and cancellations and disgraces
as the television mimes in red and yellow fire the revolution of the wet load
in the dryer. And yet the sisters Ruiz ruck the smocks and sheets
of the last-hired broker and the Boriqua and the athlete.
Cool in summer, warm in winter. The daughter does her homework
in the corner. No loitering. No dyeing. Down a flight from the whip pan
and walla of the street. Wash and fold. *Abrázame muy Fuerte.*
The lost and found holds orphaned socks. The world
should be Ruiz run, accommodating dirt, ransomed of terror
for an hour. You get twelve minutes for a quarter.

DEVOTION: HÖRLUST

Hörlust, roughly "hearing passion," pleasure in sound, but also pain
as the child Tchaikovsky weeping in his bed screams, "This music.
It's here in my head. Save me from it." His mother's voice peals
like a bell. His father's chair squeals as he rises from his meal in E
above C. . . . Save me from the run of octaves in my skull
subtle as an owl's. Save me from the door slam and the plain
song of the mosquito, the pandemonium of car alarms, the Donald
Duck of the mall, and the twelve-tone row of the adored. It's here
in my head, the tunings of the world sitar, the phrasings of the sax,
the heave'e'yo of stevedores, what Whitman had in his head with the blab
of the pave and the voice of a streetcar conductor he loved.
When it's quiet, but it's never quiet, I hear the hum or hiss, that mammal
or reptile, in the ark somewhere and the caterwaul of the pulse and the god
thud. It's in here. It's nowhere. When we wanted Manuel Noriega out
of his asylum in the diplomatic mission of the Vatican we played Van Halen's
"Panama"—*Pan-neh-mah-ah-ah, whoo*, until the Vatican complained.
They have some mortally boring nerve. Listen, it's the clamor or the aura
of the subdued you hear. A sob, a rasp, a drone. Sound the thrill,
sound the tempered clavier. A voice makes a sound tearing the air, the veil
rent, the entrails spilled. Cold is a sound you feel in your back teeth
where they stuck the needle. Still you must listen for the racket of the cricket's
front knees or the electric locks of the jail. Click in E above C. Still, but
it's never still, you must pet the cat until the cat can't stand it, the feedback
of nervous static and the self made by the loop of sensation becomes the poet
praising a god aroused to anger by the ugly and put to sleep by the beauty
of the mallet and anvil in the inner ear. There's a photo of Thelonius Monk
under the lid of a piano at Minton's, New York 1949, like a snapshot

of Hörlust. You can see he's making the sounds in his head come out
all over the staves. Offsetting the harmonies. He's leaning over
the soundboard on top of the hammers. The smoke from his cigarette
makes a long stem of a note, then something like a bass cleft.
He smoked in quarter notes and rests. His stylish attack and swell.
Man, piano, smoke—half killed by it, half wanting to kill.

DEVOTION: NEW YORK, JULY

Estas brutal, someone says about the heat or the boriqua
walking down the street with a dulce con leche. My sister
shivers. I paraphrase a fever when I mount the stairs
to the roof to swelter among the compressors and powers,
the lotus dome of exhausted air, the reedy pipes of no organ,
the Egyptian jars of water. The body is postpartum in shimmers
of tar and carbon. What's that flavor in the mouth left after
the da-dum, da-dum? Dishes spill milk and catch the chatter
of the planet bounced from desert to Sputnik to the solar
wind of wherever: there was a wire, there was a burning tire
and smoke, a sniper like a divine seen through a lens in the green
black water of night, and then boys gone to vapor in a red mist,
the body released from rumors of the precious, the glorified,
the splendid five liters. Then the condolezza of a piano
and a mother says *cocksucker* to the messengers and a lover
sings to a lover the improvised device of desire. You wanted sugar?
You wanted power? You wanted from the blood clot another
to disfigure? You stare in the window of the fifteenth floor
where a headless creature with breasts moves toward
a headless creature who receives her. Now the windows glare
and the sun bankrupts New Jersey, layers and waters
and martyrs the West. There's no end to the chatter:
From al-Mansur, *I took some shrapnel here and here.*
On my kneepads I wrote my blood type in big red letters.

DEVOTION: THIRST REDUCTION

Wherever there was water—the upended lid of a mayonnaise jar
in the gutter, the gutter, the sober silver puddle, the frenzied lake,
the tear ducts, the dew, the beveled rain—we drank. We bent down
our lips to any inscription in the stone, to any pock or V, a dog bowl
on the porch, dimple, thimble, dent, collarbone hollow. We drank
from the palm, from the philtrum—that crease in the upper lip.
We wanted it quiet or we wanted Katrina. We sipped from the trumpet
of the honeysuckle, swallowed like circus freaks the swords of the iris
down to the hilt. We drank from your high-heeled shoes. Water
to slake the American thirst in our midbrain where the American
want was. It tasted a lot like misery dissolved in joy. We hoisted
more than one in the bedroom, at the kitchen table, on the floor,
over the sink, in the parking lot of the convenience store—
our gills fanning a flame we couldn't put out. From the bubbler,
the canteen, the sippy cup, from the pool of ink, we drank.
Given our affliction anything could be juiced—a car, a daughter.
(The art of juicing isn't hard to master.). In the wider-than-the-sky
brain, there is a larger-than-yourself mouth that fastens around you
like a lover, but a brutal, stupid lover, and here comes one now
who can reach inside you to the source of terror and pleasure,
under the ribs: Adam fetching a woman: that's how it felt.
(It wasn't a disaster.) None of us had milk for the other,
mammals that we were. We were soft-skulled creatures
who cried when our ball fell down the storm sewer.
We could hear but we could not touch the fluency—
could not drink or drown, had to free ourselves
from ourselves using only our mouths.

DEVOTION: REDSHIFT

occurs when the light from an object shifts towards
the red end of the spectrum: an increase in wavelength,
a decrease in frequency. And I saw the white horse
in the fields of central New York become at sunset a fiery
red light and its rider was given the tools of shock and awe
and the power to break the seals as light from the objects
shifted and the oil wells burned on the day of shock and awe.
Once there was circumference, now the field gets red,
redder as in a room where blood spins in a centrifuge
testing the body for its red ends. Things move away
in waves. Puff and bombast, the Macbeth of things. Vision
is vivisection. Redshift: Hiroshima, 1946. And I was born
in a dilation of time as the wavelength lengthened
and the creature said, "Come and see." And I heard,
redshift, Lord Amherst say give the blankets
with the smallpox to the Indians, redshift, and let the corpses
dead of the plague be flung over the wall by a catapult, redshift,
and the Assyrians corrupt the wells and Hannibal
fill the water jars with vipers. Shock and awe.
I move away from me. Once there was a room
where I died just a little, now I'm chemical, awful,
the target of light, the target of fleas and the moon turns
blood red, light shifts, skin blisters, time dilates,
the liver swells with toxins, and the sky rolls up like a scroll,

redshift, in shock and awe. I write on my skin on the red end of the spectrum. My nation endows the chemicals that turn the skin to coal. And the sun turns black like a sackcloth made of goat hair as the oil wells burn. The vector of my life is a vesper mouse and the target is my skin. And in the fields of central New York I saw a riderless horse, a fiery red one.

DEVOTION: SMOKE

There's a game on, but there's always a game on, and a tire fire
in the distance squalling smoke in your direction and threshold
limit values of cadmium and chromium like a Mannerist painting
done in flame and volatile oils (plus benzene and coal tar and the oxides
of our recent being on earth). The tennis is sensational, isn't it?
The ground strokes, the aces, the *donc donc* like a translation of grunts
to French. Thus the American is left with love after a crosscourt
topspin, difficult to return, difficult to even reach. The sky is orange,
like a level of threat, and gray like another country—one we came from
or one we set on fire. 40—Love. We like a good game with perspiring.
Our secretary of state likes anything, she says, with a score behind it.
And behind that the perfumes of the superfluous and the shared
vapors of our ruin, and behind that a sparrow, and behind that
the work men do at the rehab because of the work men do.
(The nerve ends keep forming a man composed of nerve ends.)
The smoke smells like a French confection burnt in the kitchen
of the prison. Play continues after rain. The sky is a black rose.
The sensational moments scored for us, the sky scored for us
into the adored and uncared for and the struggle that governs
as someone faults and someone sweats and the fire governs.

DEVOTION: HIGH SCHOOL

The boys (mostly) in shop class vent the teethings of the band saw on wood
and the filings of sheet metal through the industrial exhaust fan into the Mid-
west. Silvers the lilacs. Pollinates the lakes. The boys make something
they can carry, although they carry little, like refugees, and the rest
is dust, radically empty, free, unspeakable. They hammer out a loud first
person. They like the noise, what noise? And they like the fire, swords
beat into swords. They want sugars (mostly), and oceans and orders
or the opposite, a magic that will spring them from detention.
Wanting and thinking and making make for a muchness felt
as something missing. Through their ear buds come the thuds
of African drum circles, which will make their meager peculiar
and make the high-pitched shouts of girls (mostly) rational. In their ears
emo and cash flow. The wetness of waves unseen. I can taste the dust
of their suchness. They have safeguarded themselves. I can taste
their sadness. The unmade is their beauty and their worry. They unmake
me. Because they disbelieve the world, they must make it again and again.
A table or a footstool or a stash box or a sword or a cutting board
in the shape of a whale. Busy and clever and industrious the world
and noisy with lust and exhaust. Because they are instructed loudly
and told to wise up and no handguns or cell phones they become wordless
(mostly) except for the recitative of the engines and the drums in their ears.
Because it will end in June, they will make it endless. They will alter
the mufflers. They will modify the fenders and the first person.
Because somebody knows somebody who lost a finger to the saw,

they will be unable to imagine more than 9 deaths. The Tutsis,
The Armenians, the Jews will be unimaginable. They have the second
and third persons to suffer through right now, a class in Thou and It,
as they are in the Middle Passage, the Trail of Tears, and wanting,
like the drums say, a woman (mostly) to tell the whole story,
to put their mouths on what's yet to be said.

DEVOTION: HUNAN HOUSE

How did we know the rooms, the ones with the Persian
rugs and dust, salukis, and prerevolutionary violins,
would be visited again in Anniston, Alabama and then
in the closets of the Red Roof Inn? The old rooms had Ornette,
had cinderblocks (for ballast) and books: *Love's Body* and *Affluence
to Praxis*, we read until we thought we were classless. We cooked
on the filaments of the hot plate rigged over the tub, a hell-bent,
death-kissed breakfast. We had too much skin, too much grease
to be god-forsaken. Something we wanted that wasn't sex
or work made us leave the rooms and be in New York
where we were the squires of smoke, redistributed princes
of science. We wanted something from the pot liquor
and the cured meats that wasn't home. In our Russian period
we wore our father's overcoats and listened to the race stations
to get the butter of the soul. What if the soul, says B, is unspeakable
except in time? Not ecstasy but a musical history? But
what if it's all chemical, says A, and works on the same principle
as sea bass and chilies with enzymes and acids? What if beauty
gets chewed and moves from solid to chyme to gut to
the ruminated gift of molecule and heat? I don't think the spirit
comes from inside, says B, like a sweat. We come alive agonized.
Noah unloads the ark, then Syria, Persia, Rome, the fucking
Turks, death marches and genocide, that's the soul: to survive
three thousand years to lick the garlic sauce off our lips.

DEVOTION: SOUP

"And who, I wonder, was the man that was not content to prepare
himself by hunger only for the satisfying of a greedy appetite?"
—Pliny, *Natural History*

Wanting to use everything, wanting to be beautifully used . . .
Rind, pith, placenta, the orts, the scourings, the skimmed
solids, skin rotted and bruised because of you and September.
The globe of the peach has its North America darkened, sweet,
too sweet, and I eat it on my way to other eating, pleasure monster
that I am. The juice of first one, then two hemispheres
devoured and then no place to stand and nowhere to put the lever.
Nothing eats me but the space between the kill, the soup,
the spill where I am perpetual and *Spices fly at the receipt,*
said Dickinson, *it was the distance was savory.* Pick out
the loose stones and sticks and soak the peas an hour.
Combine mung beans, sprouts, chili, and the ghee—
what was stolen from the gods, call it sap, call it the weeping
body, call it butter, it also means desire, the semiliquid way to love
the thing that's not, heat and ingredient thieved and received,
then add turmeric and asafetida—devil's dung, the root
that smuggled fire from the gods, cook an hour
and add the carrots and cauliflower in florets, red radishes,
boil and then simmer gently for two or three minutes
to prevent burning. Haven't you been taken by the flame?
Haven't you confused the fire and the song about the fire?
Sprinkle coriander, cumin, garam masala. The poem used

to mask the rot of meat and nations lost and found
on the umbrels of a small flower. Add black pepper
for empire. Add salt, for a man in love lives in a salted state,
the Romans thought, and so to engross the present
and sit with my hunger and be mulligatawny,
add the rest of the coriander in a steamy blue bowl.

DEVOTION: FORT DRUM

I don't know if it meant collusion (to play together), corruption,
complicity (to fold together), or duplicity (to fold twice), some
venality in the knowledge, in the skill (it was for sale, it was technical),
some crime, fraud, futility (we lost), a breach of trust, but I was a coach.
I made the children run and stop. I made them watery and sincere.
I made them chase balls like pups and told them a taller, faster man/
woman would have had it. I told them to defend themselves,
duck, dodge, fake, bluff, trap, feint, act, fool. I made them
devoted and naked and famous for a second in their forms.
And then the nurslings, the nestlings went off to their endeavors, wet-
haired, bruised, but not beaten, defending themselves. Went off
to juvenile, to juco, to father's business or Jesus, went off
to Fort Drum, home of the 10th Mountain Division where they learned
Loyalty, Duty, Respect, Honor, Integrity, Personal Courage—
what I did not teach them. Nor did I build character. And from Fort Drum
came back damaged and disfigured, grieved in their bodies and their skin
was different. Some cold. Escorted by men in full dress, ribbons,
braid, medals who learned taciturn to honor them and I'm all horror
of a mother who gets the knock on her door and her green gray
life is a blur until they hand her a flag in a triangle. Honor and horror.
The two theaters of the same American brain that monsters
nightmare and character, fever and power, martyrs
belief. I knew what it took to beat the spurious, treacherous out
of my system by sitting, by davening, by learning to be a woman,
shunting the terrible and beautiful, and why the tutelary
gods slept outside my door as I dreamed I was in the mud
of a day after rain in October and the children were romping
and next to me was a stern man with a German name concerned
with loss. I crawled forward in a field of crosses.

DEVOTION: MEDEA

After the divorce I was a white witch fated with madness
which was a rich chemical maleness—an aroma of harm
around me like the civet of a cloudy leopard. I alarmed
myself. I was a man and a soul that loves what leaves me
hates the pleasure that's the kitchen, wants the sublime.
Who hasn't conjured up a poison dress, magnificent
in virility, a cloak of the shaman's whose desires were a kiss
into submission, woman into man and disturbing distances?
I was relentless and resentful, both synonyms of the hours
I spent manufacturing mayhem to myself or spells on others
who tried to help. I didn't need help . . . I needed fuel and air.
I padded around in my bathrobe in the Very Rich Hours
of my fear and read Baudelaire and watched wrestling
just for the obvious and excruciating virtues and the beating
I could see was phony, but so was matrimony. And then it wasn't
funny. I lost the end of my nose. I looked like a sugar skull
on Dia de Los Muertos. I sent the kids back to her every Monday—
my besneakered babies, my two betrayers—with a hat
she'd forgotten or a negligee she left in the laundry
when she used to stay. Oh used. Oh used to. I said sotto voce
burn to death and then it was I went up in flames
and the others whose names I called when they loved me
were casualties of the necromancy I cast by saying back
the word *love*. Then I killed the kids with my sword.

DEVOTION: RED ROOF INN

Write like a lover. Write like you're leaving yourself for another.
Write like you're de Beauvoir, object and subject. Write
like you must rescue yourself from yourself, become scrupulous
to the body and the rain that floods you with rage and the crude
sublimities: there was a lip print on the plastic glass wrapped
in the misty domestic interior of the room. Write like there's evidence,
there's tenderness, like Paris were the scene of a crime. A lipstick
by the bed, a phone number, a plastic glass with prints. The remote
is toxic. At the Red Roof Inn they couldn't recommend an alternative
to suffering. Like lovers we spoke of short term/long term knowledge—
and the rest in the circle of hell the telephone allows. *I want
my piracy*, I thought you said. The familiar doesn't travel well.
The soul doesn't travel well. Poetry spoils. Write like you're Mingus.
Write like the evidence vanishes. Inflammable walls between devoted
ghosts—smoke and the convention of the fourth wall pulled down.
Drama majors, drum majors next door, the all-night opera with starling
sounds. The Red Roof Inn hath me in thrall. The highway sounds
like the sea in storm, pirates with their perishable cargoes.
Their ship goes down. The soul doesn't travel well. Write
like the ship goes down with your belongings. Write like you're in thrall.
We're blown around like Paola and Francesca, lovers, carnal,
windy starlings, misled by the sublime—the binge and purge
of the book and the body. I'm wildly attracted to you winter and fall
when I fly the migration routes from Corpus Christi to Saint Paul.
Or is that summer? I do not travel well. I travel like a lover,
boy king or saboteur, stormed by the fluids of the body.
I'm wildly attracted to your feathers, your lip and book.
My greatest vows are in the getting out. I kneel to look under
the bed for belongings. I've pirated myself. Thank you for the chance

to fly, the leaving. Thank you for the soft pink tissue, your cargo
of ghosts. The telephone is toxic. The body's a rumor. The leaf
blower in the opera is over the top. Thank you for the brimming.
Thanks for the speech acts and action, the alternative to suffering.
Sorry for the hoarse sobs. I'm wild about the red noise of the traffic,
the holy wars of the starlings. Flying back all the songs are of glistening.
Flying back the passenger in 5D is unwilling to rescue others, unwilling
to rescue himself. Write like you've lost your belongings.

DEVOTION: GUITAR

From Tuscaloosa west to Mississippi then north to Memphis
through country as unmusical as I was unloved by the decorous

ardor of the South and the voice of one whose griefs
were Cherokee, absentee, left in the Chevy and secret.

She didn't love my love like Shiva's everywhere and blue
and many-handed, some with knives and some with billet-doux.

She wouldn't sacrifice the better judgment I'd want of her.
Like stopped clocks (black hands, white faces) the geographic cure

was true two times a day. All time else I was wrong
and blued like the notes of the guitar, drum, saxophoned songs

I was receiving: a magnet wound around a steel coil—
a Les Paul—the quavers I converted to an electric boil

that simmered into the sweet, fry-oil air.
I can be mortified anywhere, everywhere.

DEVOTION: THE BURNT-OVER DISTRICT

Late fall in the villages of Pompey, Oran, Delphi Falls, churched
river and woods. In Homer and Ovid, the localities and principalities
of central New York, the hollows and corners of the burnt-over
districts visited by angels in the 1800s who led us to greatness:
gold, awakenings, portents and lies, heaven, women's suffrage,
and bundling with the other in the love beds while we waited
for the lamb, the dove, the velvet of the ten-point buck grunting
through the underbrush to rut. We learned in divine time
a year's a day. We learned obedience and had charismatic children.
And now the boy's an angelic eighteen days or six thousand years,
as he leaves to serve. He did what we told him: blocked for punts—
no one likes to block for punts—and when his friends crashed
the truck in a ditch, he waited for the cops and took the rap,
nice kid, because he did the act of deliverance one does
in central New York and made the vows, pledged, testified, and swore
and played (and was) a sport greater than the coming of the dead,
and escorted the exaggerated girl to the prom where he was befuddled
with organza and tulle and he did not forget the corsage, an orchid
in a box he stared into: the white outer whorl and the inner whorl
and pouted purple lip. He butterflied the pollen with the lashes
of his eyes. The flower was his terror. He was not meant to be
the indwelling beauty of things and surely he was not meant to be
the wind in Iraq with three others in his division and become
the abstract shape of a god formed from a blood clot.
I've seen the pictures, the vague shapes that ripple in the heat.
It looked like he still moved. Remember fall in Delphi?
All ardent and catastrophic and counter, elbows flailing,
he ran in the flat places scraped from the gold hills and valleys.

DEVOTION: DUB

After the jets crashed into the buildings and the buildings
came down without my figures of speech and the people I knew
died with lipsticks in their purses and lottery tickets in their pockets,
I walked the slave paths through the scrub oaks of Alabama
and walked down 9th Avenue past the sidewalk art and psychics
and went home, wherever that was, with the hot, thick
tears that poets and lovers shed to the angina of Philadelphia
where speech was distressed and loudmouthed and failed to shape
up anything and my grievances failed and hate failed and I waited
for the paddles to be pressed against my hearts by CNN. My hearts—
self-indulgent, self-delighting, cumbersome, rank—a pack of hounds
loosed in Philadelphia, Tuscaloosa, and the capoeria of New York—
the backlash of back matter making a new memory out of snarls
and barks. I moved. In the new house I bought hangers and shelf paper
and new pillows for the mercy seat, and fueled the seven lamps
with seven lips. I made a living. I blinked. I started to collect crumbs.
I started a song cycle. First the syntax of the body, then feeling,
then love reassembled out of the tar bubbles, a biscuit odor and the mind
flooded by fear where the high-water marks are recorded and dubbed
like an EKG of my hearts' headway. Open up my hearts and there
are twenty-six dead today—I don't know their names in Arabic—
and in another heart the words of the song dropped out and the drum
turned up so it's just *lub-Dub, lub-Dub*. Not just. Never just.
The beat, the bass is everything. There were trees. There were oaks
blowing in Alabama like a nerve network, druids fingering the breeze.
And in Philadelphia an inner room where light on the wall was left over
from informing others, a used, ancestral, rumor. Light like some geometry
that's also some abiding. Light's body English. Between the trees
and the lighted room, a woman sits at an upstairs window. Stressed,

unstressed, which is it? The answer is unstressed, stressed. Vision
the syntax of everything. She's either the light's opus or one
of the beats of one of my hearts. Memory forgives itself for the hearts'
atrocities, the axes the hearts flourished as they hacked their way
through the thicket, south, then north. Now the surge.
Now the terror. Now everyplace I see is somewhere else.

DEVOTION: OBBLIGATO

Late August was a pressure drop,
rain, a sob in the body,

a handful of air
with a dream in it,

summer was desperate
to paradise itself with blackberry

druplets and swarms, everything
polychromed, glazed, sprinkler caps

gushing, the stars like sweat
on a boxer's skin. A voice

from the day says
Tax cuts

for the rich or *scratch*
what itches or it's a sax

from Bitches Brew,
and I'm confused

by these horns
and hues, this maudlin

light. It's a currency of feeling
in unremembered March.

There's a war on and snow in the city
where we've made our desire stop

and start. In the dying school of Bruce
I'm the student who still believes

in the bad taste of the beautiful
and the sadness of songs

made in the ratio
of bruise for bruise.

DEVOTION: RENT

I'd like the mannerists and the brutalists better if they began
their ventures, *rent due*. I'd like the ironists and the sincere better too.
And the white people and the new metaphysicians and the friends
of the rain. So, rent due. Leaf drop. The last stoop sitting
of the summer. The last of the new jack swing. The muted trumpet
and the scalded maple are either absolutes or references. Who knows
what music means? The rain begins in irony, ends in sincerity,
a devotion to darkening, a policy of tiny, shining rivers. We expect
a blues from the rain and get it—buck, buck, bail—the rent
come due. There's a deep wish I have to see the beautiful losers
in the postseason taking their futile swings—a kind of politics,
a kind of blindness, a brain without estrogen. Whose bitch am I?
Exorbitant, the rents. Unlivable. The sincere are forced to live
in brutal elsewheres, to pay and pay. I contribute "as I am able"
to child support. The boy on the subway asks in all sincerity,
"Do I look rich?" to the other hostages to oblivion. They'll grow
brutal. Who but the ironic can afford to live here, and why can't
the reckoning of living be Dickinson and Langston Hughes,
whose rent was due? Ask the landlords. Ask the white people.
Ask the rain. She got on at Columbus Circle and I could not read
The Taoist Body for wanting to look at her and not look at her
and thereby save her from the past two thousand years of eye rage
and shame. Years of bucking and bailing, shimmy and obey. I look
away, a kind of blindness. The boys do a heel-toe slide beat-boxing
our Grandmaster Flash. The boys do the drum machine and samples
of our great god Brown. I look. A book is a child I must support,
a solitary child with a scar. She got off at 116th—she had on only
metaphysical clothes, her legs scraped clean of the mammal in stappy
black things. Music's a motive. Rent's a consequence. Coming into

the station light takes its swings artfully, artlessly. Sometimes I feel rent
by the music, sometimes sustained. Sometimes I feel like
a motherless child. I stood up and my lap vanished. Everywhere
a miasma and fictional mooring of desire and father. This token
is good if you're white and rich. In the trash—a crutch,
a mattress, a cymbal. What more do I need? A book, twelve bars
of the brutal, and rent money. And music to be made as I am able.

DEVOTION: DIZZY GILLESPIE

Half what you make of it and half envy and fear and the rest
living in the world, buying a lottery ticket and a coffee to go
while anointing with your oil the face of the one you love
then the faces of all those you love while you're loving
the one you love. Each heartbeat a betrayal of the dead
second you just loved a second ago. Ghost maker, ghost
fucker, ghost eraser. There's a hurt behind the eyes and a sick
series of recriminations accompanied by hard-consonant
Anglo-Saxon words. In other words, she loves you not.
Money laundered, cat gutted, day extinguished, the face
effaced. And yes, you wrote bad checks but the extravagant
number of zeroes stands for the excess of your love
as does the singing of the *Song of Songs* to both of them
and the same flowers beheaded on her behalf also murdered
for another: La Rêve—the nodding blood-spattered lily,
a pink illuminated by an oily sunset, sepals and petals curved
backwards like necks arching until they touch the stem.
You're driving. It's December. You pull in stations
from Toronto and Mexico, faithless in your frequencies
in the dark. You get the faint signal from New York. It's Dizzy
playing beyond his death the bop Latin brash sweetness,
or one-tenth of him from the extravagant cheeks to electrons
in your cortex. It's him and the absence of him in the anvil
and stirrup of the inner ear. The anvil forging the wheel

as if for the first time and the stirrup he puts his foot in
and presses against his instep and takes you
to a place where the fugitive surrenders
to what happens and the betrayal itself is betrayed
in the four seconds it takes to forget,
but I don't forget you, ghosts.

DEVOTION: J'S DREAM

I dreamed I was able to bridge the distance between
the brains and the tits and woke as if in a soft document
of mercy, sheets, snow, and something unseen making away,
wings making the air sulky and cold. Wait. I beseeched you.
I was able to reach across the breach between Marianne Moore
and John Berryman, between your odd, spylike gaze
and erudition and the nut and rut of me. Come back.
You had such lovely dreams you could not restrain:
we were at war and you were in a plane, a little rusty reddish one,
when the plane ahead of you dives with that revving fading engine
noise and you were thinking how much harder it is to go first
telling yourself you are going to die as you were falling
on a sortie slipstream lazy eight Mayday yaw and roll.
The plane ahead of you got tiny, a tiny red dot
then a spark like from an emery wheel just a single flit
and then you're on the ground where everything was quiet.
The daylight gray white hard to tell dusk or dawn no sight
of the enemy but these husks or hulks of downed planes
like mastodon skeletons in and around the frames of a ruined
building but even the ruins were shiny new with torn white walls
like new paper, wood that's fresh and bright as snow—
like the pith from a broken-off willow, and you're thinking
how strange this mix of right now and ruined
still, you're on the wrecked and open sill of a window
on the third floor, but at that story you can't tell
if it's under construction or it's under destruction
when you see someone in a hat, a curved better version

of me as a woman although my eyes are Xed when I turn
to face you. We're both tremendously happy
although you are worried about my eyes,
and you turn to me speaking from business documents
and schoolbooks while I can only sing a blues
about the rules for distance and difficult love.

DEVOTION: AL GREEN

I rode the Greyhound watching the twitchy things of the North give way
to the sticky, bloodshot things of the South. No ground so burnt
there's not a church where I heard the Reverend amplify, rarefy,
and glorify the word so that we were all in some state of sweating July.
The ashy black man and the white bail bondsman held each other
until they were blue. I heard the Reverend take the hymn of my mama
and the whore's perfume and mix them. Downhome/downtown.
His voice in Arkansas behind the plow. His voice in Michigan stoop sitting.
His voice in a satin cheap tuxedo as he drew back from the microphone
and in the air the tea olive bloomed—formal, miraculous pockets of sweetness
I turned to. . . . Now, his voice soars over the devil in falsetto, finding the register
that floats me over the sugar hill and the narrow path. I'm falling into the hands
of a man who vows never to let go as he lowers me (his breath on my face)
into the river—Reverend, I will not throw the scalding grits in your face.
I just want the blush from your stubble, and *here I am Baby*
to be kindled by your body.

DEVOTION: PARIS

I knew people who knew people who knew Gertrude Stein
and said they helped themselves to cake, drank a glass of wine
from the glasses lined up on the credenza when life was a young
Beaujolais, then laughed with the ambulance driver. Danger, ha.
Terror, pft. But not I. I spent my days here in the hotel room
where pleasure is revealed as a brooding in the body and brooding
is revealed as *a cloud, a shame, all that bakery can tease,* Stein said
either laughing or brooding. The body is a breeze and nirvana
means *to cease blowing,* as a candle broods, flickers, feasts on nothing.
From here I can see steps down to the Seine like the gray sheets
I pull off the bed to wrap around me and become the deranged water
I must brood over. About sheets: I am the spill and the snarl
of their knotting, their drape and blotting all that abounds.
I am the bodhisattva of sheets, an American come here to learn
to see inly. Shut the blinds. I'm learning to see at the red end
of the spectrum through the louvers of the jalousie that scores
the bed with bars of light and dark. About color:
I am the ambulance driver. I carry a body in its bloody sheet
or carry a space for a body back and forth. There's a war.
I slow the spirit, move the matter, dye the room a roast beef color.
The floor, the sheets, the dirty water, the gray spaces out the window
are the membrane of a dream I can't remember.
I am the thickly painted dusk of summer
where Americans come to dip their toes. . . . About her:
she teases me into ceasing. Out of our enchantments, *real cadence
and a quiet color,* Stein said. She sugars me in her being. She breezes
me. She forgives me my state. She feeds me a little something,
maybe some mutton, maybe just a piece of cake.

DEVOTION: CONTRABAND

That thing you sent didn't open,

didn't change my life as it should, didn't complicate,

or play, although it made a hate

crime, a love note—both of those—a stolen

thing from the Congo passed through France

then shown to Picasso by Matisse at Stein's apartment

a carving, a mask, a dance—a misrepresented

soul that became the thing—a trance

we lived in while we built the Great Wall,

The Chrysler Building, the Erie Canal—servants

to the civilization, dowsing, digging,

never stopping to drink. God strangled

the details as we smuggled the cargoes

of our gifted lives, our lies, our singing.

DEVOTION: NEW YORK, 1970

In the singing school there were weepholes
and rats, preternatural creatures in sequins who spoke a Creole

no one understood. There was a pain threshold
feedback from the amps. There were harlequin opals

in the navels. There were flames
of cellophane the exhaust fan flamed.

I behave like what I am—a legitimate gypsy
said Lorca's shadow leaving St. Marks-in-the-Bowery.

In the work and underwork of the coat closet
you were rubbed in fur and worsted.

There was a narcoleptic Juliet on a balcony
your voice annoyed. There was archeology

in the twice-cooked pork, cultures in the cheeses.
Instead of character you had disease.

There was a mime of the holocaust
in your run for the bus.

Then you went through tunnels saying
"In-a-Gadda-Da-Vida, Baby,"

and came out blinking like Plato.
The burden of autumn sun, sparrows,

sophomores and young execs, arrogant
humble people who would whine and rant

and you, cynical and triumphantly
getting by without soul, without dancing, without l-u-v.

DEVOTION: JOSEPHINE P

She enters the ciphers of November, the trees
that eat the lime like Emma Bovary.

She enters the waters of the Charles
the missing chord of shadows, the snarls

of light. Six months since she was kissed horizontal—
from June's trance to the brutal miracle.

She enters as one enters a house in a fairy tale
to dream and serve the great god of details

by becoming one. A button of blood shoved
through a hole in the sheets that someone loved

but not me, not me, not me
(But still she moves.)

I could live forever had I not looked
at her like a glyph in an Egyptian book

I could not read. I begin the séance of broad day—
a coffee, a token, a ride on the subway—

holding no other hands, no table, no candles
flickering, no voices, no veil

rent by my looking at the things:
the dogs and money and glittering earrings.

for my mother, Josephine Preston Smith

DEVOTION: CHANGELING

I backed away from the revolving door to let the man
stir himself in. He looked like he had served two-thirds of his time,
(I had worked at Lewisburg. I knew an ex-con
when I saw one)—and now was on parole, careful to defer to the pushy,
the striving, the vaulting who have inherited the earth since his send up
for his crimes. He had been, in my mind, among the slightly more vicious,
fraudulent, and unruly, and thank Bush for jails. I looked up at him
who was looking at me, a man my age, my changeling, with a face
come into the face he deserved at sixty, a felonious face shadowed there,
inside the building and wearing clothes I once wore, but shabbier, dingier,
the worse for wear, and around him a caged halo like submarine creatures
have in dense refracted light. I hated that it was myself, my effigy,
as it was what I hated in my father, the deferential smile, the waiting,
the severe and saddening self-sense of place, and his wish, his devotion,
to taking up as little space as possible, his tiny shoes, living his life
in perpetual fall in the elementary school among children and the small
splendors of seeds in cups and glittered, crayoned skies that get obliterated
here in the lobby of the Federal building where marshals back
from a tour of Iraq trigger my fight or flight and whisper
Sunni and *Shiite* as I work my way in and let the man out to his birthright.

DEVOTION: THE GARMENT DISTRICT

In bed as the machinery of morning begins, indistinguishable
the subterranean turbines of the A train from the jet engine
as it gins the clouds, rips and reseams the length of denim
on its way to Pittsburgh (with the terrible and subtle cargoes,
with ashes and a cat under the seat) from the pulleys
of the service elevators from the baffled sound across the alley
of the hand-iron press and the sewing machine motors whirring
bobbins that stitch together the hot properties of Seoul, the suburbs
and the idiot village of Chelm, needle the veronica and the Buddha
robe and the sateen for spring. I looked over at her. Her skin
a warp of ghost and a weft of meat. All night she had hauled
me and the boy, and the smoky, feckless men I was across
the fens and stretches of mesquite through the tunnels
and delivered me to my misery and the laborious knots of the sheets
I wound myself in. And she was exhausted from Eros and swollen
from anger. She could stand to put on a few pounds. I could see it
in her ribs. Before I would marry my restlessness to her terror,
before the crushes and wages could be made into our equity, before
the endlessness would end in spinning jennies and sleaze and the noise
of a fleet of vehicles with tinted windows testing the evacuation routes,
I would cut, then peel, then dice, then caramelize some onions
before she wasted away to nothing.

DEVOTION: *WUTHERING HEIGHTS*

The obliteration of snows, all the letters deposed, then effaced,
from the (   ) scape, no pleasures or all
the below zero refusals, now the crows like justices X-Oed.
So thoroughly in the body (in the wind) there was hardly
any room for a splinter of nonbody to be slipped (a long
syllable like an acupuncture needle) in—like driving a shaft
of straw through a telephone pole as I heard hurricanes can do
by the heel of a god hand or by voodoo (or a voice) push—
(I said I *saw* her in concert but I only slightly heard)—
and then I felt as the body stumbles, swerves to avoid itself
in time that the voice is a woman's and the hand is my brother's
as he unloads cargo from the docks where bodies are stacked,
locked up, iced down, gassed (no tarantulas, ripens the fruit),
pumped, spread, as the salts from Korea deliquesce.
He was blue from the stowing, rich from the overtime and ripe
for the nonbody to pierce his palms as he unloaded the sides
of beef from Argentina, some peaches on pallets with winches.
The gift of the stevedore is the gift of the dreamer: to nurse
our need (and so what if we lose a little something in the handling:
some dust, a Volkswagen?). To be so thoroughly in the body was
to hide the desolation in the devotion like Heathcliff to Catherine
(whose heart beats *visibly and audibly),* and Catherine to Heathcliff
with his brutal, Marxist/Capitalist whip hand, until that voice
(I heard her slightly, but that doesn't mean I wasn't cleaved)
was familiar. Of course they were brother and sister, Heathcliff—
the dirty urchin brought home with the whip and the busted violin
to punish and fret the body of the other) so all the vows of XY
to XX and vice versa—doomed, a fatal hetero sickness, taboo,
yearning, please, blowjobs begged for, sonnets, love knot tied up

in love knot, we'll never get it right: hence the voices in the night
trying again and again, darling, *I wanna know what love is . . .*
I invited the splinter (the spider) in, the way a splitting wedge
(one short stroke) laid across the rings of pith invites the V
in the name of a willingness to kill (a voice is laid across a body
while the signatures of time pass through). While over the radio
the songs you can't turn off, over 141 covers and versions
from schmaltz to African drums, power ballads, jerk songs, karaoke
to yodels to hums. My brother, my blue obliterated dreamer, the stuff
is stuffed (the stevedores have broken for lunch), the body is split
and stacked, corded and lugged, and there's something lost, of course,
maybe a language (we grunt and puff), but what's that voice?
A child singing? A crow? Lovers calling to each other across the snows?

DEVOTION: SLEEP

He dreamed his face was lashed by waves he split as the masthead
of a ship, a leaking vessel, *The Idiot Pirate*. She slept as if she were
taunted by borrachos with guns and knives who made her dance,
"Dance muchacha." Each night he medicated himself with oxygen
against living in the world with or without women. If only
her lousy six hours of blindfolded flailing were death kiss, death
spread, but waking and living was failing to die and so the sorrow
as the rain carried the news of the jihad and the Al-Jezeera
stills to them as well as the triumphs of art
and love and so the ardor and the fury and sleep a style
that counters and encounters forgeries of the received.
At night their chests pull in like millions of Americans.
The sensation is choking, is waking up in order to breathe,
many awakenings without Zen. His REM became his waking state.
Her body went rag doll on her. Like millions of Americans, there was
a delay in the signals from the brain. The whole country was corpses
and body parts and restless leg and vivid dream. On the brink
of falling asleep while swimming, while laughing, while angry.
We were laughing and angry and collapsed into the numinous
poles and dark continents. Bring the jaw forward, darling,
elevate the soft palate, retain the tongue. If our poetry can't be
sweet and useful, we must sleep our deformed sleep. In his dream
he held her hand as at a séance and outside the street wind-blown
with promo leaflets, faces like seeds from a glamorous tree
naked in its need to be seen. In her dream the guts of the puppies
were outside their bodies, giving the world its difficulty to be
loved unconditionally, giving the world its bad name.

DEVOTION: BUS TO UTICA

.

Waiting on a bench like the one outside the third grade classroom
where you were sent for singing badly or like the disinfected slab
at the clinic waiting for blood to be drawn. Maybe we'll have experience,
you tell me, or if not experience, time with freezing rain and Dickinson's
discs of snow. A white wait as in an unwritten poem that dreams
the crimes and kindness done to us. We're here for the distance.
Beside us a man recovered from experience who has mastered
pain and deadpan as he was mastered by his disease. Does the bus stop
in Albany? Another waiting one of us is boy with an empty sleeve
and a sulky girl born in Rome, schooled in Geneva—all Europe
went into her making, all experience teased from her, blood drawn
from her by the sky. Is this the bus to Troy? A bent-over white man leaks
from plastic bags of tropical fish: neons and guppies, clown
and tiger barbs. When he drank he opened his mouth
sometimes to water, sometimes to air, sometimes to god,
his mind leaking silver or purple like an oil spill in the canal.
We make our meek adjustments, because the bottom of the sea is cruel,
he writes on the bus stop wall, those words from Hart Crane in pencil.
He works his imaginary glove waiting for the inning to end. Find a vein
and draw experience. Smoking is how the bus is provoked. I hope,
I hope. Stop it, already, with the hopes. An upstate Juliet waits.
She is partly sunny. Does the bus stop in Verona? Does it stop
for a fifteen-minute break from experience? We'll go through
cities of one feeling, towns thin as angelfish, deadpan
villages. Cut open Dickinson and you'll find the blues, you tell me.
Kiss Dickinson and you'll find distance. Does the bus stop
at Wellbutrin? I can't draw, but you can. If the bus goes through

Mexico are we Mexicans? You draw a sketch of a Cadillac
convertible, top down, (it's not all representational):
Elvis drives into the horizon. All the cut open
and unkissed gather around. You've drawn yourself
in the backseat, smiling, quiet so as not to annoy Mr. Presley.
Cut open Elvis and you'll find a small town boy singing badly.

for Michael Burkard

DEVOTION: PROVIDENCE

What kind of Providence was it that gave tax breaks to delirium
and discipline, but left me in the wash of harsh chemicals
of feeling and a mind like the Exxon *Valdez* that spilled that year
11 million gallons of crude into the sound? Heavy sheens of oil
in my dream. Seabirds and otters, seals and eagles dead, drowned
in their own wet silhouettes. Downtown the river was paved over
then dug up and set on fire, Fridays, when Puccini blared
from the loud speakers, *Nessun dorma, Nessun dorma,* and nobody slept.
Everybody's dream transferred like currency into the river,
then set on fire in little pyres by the mayor whose unctions
were Venetian. Tax breaks for strippers and business stiffs.
That year I walked downtown into the volatile markets
of starlings, the mergers and acquisitions at Lupo's Heartbreak Hotel,
the oil money injected by Dubai. By the liquidated river,
I sat down and wept. At the intersection of Hope and Power
I was colonized and made my way into Narraganset Bay
and then into the sound. Without her I stopped depicting things.
So narcissistic in sorrow, I saw myself in bank windows
and in the river and in the fire. In dream I tried to clean
the feathers of a murrelet, held, like shadows, the necks of loons.
Cormorants coughed up a slimy likeness of her while the waters
burned. I lost irony and looked for it a half hour at a time
in the coffee shops and living rooms of *Seinfeld.*
My punishment was teaching poetry. I cried
the clothes off strippers who slid down poles like firefighters.
One was, Ladies and Gentleman, Miss Mystery. In Venice,
the punishment for crimes was either open—
the gates exposed to citizens looking in your windows, citizens
in your kitchen tasting your sauces—or shut, the damp

asylum of the self where nobody sleeps. In Providence, on the hill,
there was no end to the delirium, no end to the spillage, and no accounting
for the devotion I had to TV reruns as they were depicted by the loveless,
feckless, infantile schlubs whose motto was *no hugging, no learning.*
A tear is an intellectual thing, I said Blake said. Teaching was
stand-up that wasn't funny, exposure and quarantine. On the hill,
everyone was Shelly, nineteen, pretty, watery, and either fascist
or revolutionary. That year I walked downtown to Fellini's for a slice.
In dream, I could not undo the seabirds from their shadows. "Dying
is easy, comedy is hard," I said but did not know who said it.

DEVOTION: SYRACUSE

A siren from the telescoping wand along the boulevard
like the helical sound that flourished in the penitentiary each noon—
a test, a terror flower, a question: Who's out? Who's in?

Not a siren but a dial tone.

The Mistress of Salt says, *Did I say you could undress? What*
just fell out of your pocket? Is that your dirty penny?
Pick up your dirty penny. Put it in your mouth.
Keep it there, under your tongue, until I tell you you can spit it out.

The city's speech a slow oxidizing fire not fierce enough to burn you,
not fiery enough to keep you warm.

In dream the body was a seedpod—pericarp and placenta of the sweet flag
and not the dead come home to Fort Drum in camo body bags.

The dream was a tango in a ballroom in a strip mall.

A lacquered black Camaro in a bra.

Shadowless winter of cough and cough syrup and books
of matches like a lab for cooking crystal meth.

In dream the voice said, "Sweat the fence."

Eight months without you taught me nothing, Mistress.
Fear filled with savage self-love: my fearlessness.

Night the black corner of a Caravaggio and time/space spilled
into the room in which we watched as in a baroque zoom
lens St. Thomas stick his finger in the wound.

The Mistress says: "More witness, more style, more plot, more salt."
You love the tug on the thread as she sews your mouth shut.

The righteous don't dream and the dreamers can't start a fire
in a box of paper with a pack of matches and a butane torch.

The Mistress says more story: more amorous plural, cruising
the boulevard loving the anonymous bruising.

Your voice a creole of Utica and Rome, deer blowing,
the brakes of the bus to Toronto, the dialect
from the diaspora, the patois of cold war radio.

Bosnian dance troupe in the strip mall.
Sudanese boys on their knees in motels.

Sulk and snow like a pill crushed into a powder and snorted
that makes us ghosts and bits of gristle.

The Mistress says, "Less mystical, more mongrel."

DEVOTION: SYRACUSE EN ROSE

A city of fugues without a skeleton —Lorca

There's a bakery we can walk to for rolls hot out of the oven,
as in a Raymond Carver story, with big cups of café con leche
made Cuban style or there ought to be.

Something of July, something from the hedges
and hot patches that smells like the cologne
of Philadelphia.

An old lithograph of a view from a hill.
A sketch of a half-effaced dream
of a saint or a she-male.

Something from the spud wrench, the deep throated socket,
something of the deadblow hammer, something of the whetstone,
Skil saw, rip saw, reciprocating and saber.

The ballad of the gypsy waitress:
     I married a fire
     fighter. My dowry was water. My baby
     burns inside me without tears. Now in Albany,
     I'm dancing. It's not really about the belly.
     It's about the hips. It's about a wound to a rose.

Some wind from the Midwest, some vowel from the north,
something country—buck fever, something city—
the fall away jump shot bricks the rim.

Some afterlife in the cornices and volutes.
Some pernicious kiss, some kill grief, some limbic system,
here in the church basement, here in Adult World.

Something of clemency, something of pity
of the fleeing from Troy, something unspeakable
in the rose garden, something redeemed from the rust.

Song of the salax (the man in love):
        I was salted, Miss Bliss, and I was licked.
        Oh, I was salted and I was licked.
        In the salt city, pretty mama.
        I was the bones that you picked.

DEVOTION: DRESS

"I wasn't afraid of beauty and in fact wore beautiful things"
—Robin Behn

Beautiful dresses foreground and background: that's what the movie was
all about—although anyone could see it was about inventing the soul
by taking love to task—how love looks, subdued, stylized over time,
when it becomes a casualty of itself—if what it is about ever resides
fully in the film of things. There were dresses framed by doorways
(where we ran to in the earthquake to model our catastrophe).
There were dresses seen in hallways—red against a lacquered apple
green or green against a Tibetan red (which transforms the delusion
of attachment into the wisdom of discernment and represents
the tongue). Kimonos in fine brocades with mandarin collars.
A blue dress on a rooftop against a flinty night sky, the neon faltering,
the dress anxious as the actress smokes up a storm. Clothes
are the strangeness of the body asleep with its leprosy and dreams.
"A manifold cunning Victory over Want," Carlyle said.
Want puts on clothes, but Victory steps into and out of a dress.
Please, unzip me. What makes the dress beautiful if bias cut,
or what's stylish or altogether not, I don't know, and of the circular,
pleated, tiered and trumpeted, which is best? Empire? Shift?
Is it the figure of oppression to be ripped or the cover of the sisterhood?
What do the fissures and the slits in the kimono mean? "Matter exists
spiritually," Carlyle thought, but thought itself is an excess:
an embroidered form with a lot of language, some Scottish,
some Xhosa, and a premise that what we put on isn't really us,
but a feeling we found. The *I* is a burlesque, a measure of skin
or a bag of sweetbreads. The dress is the body's velocity. I pit this

dress against the missing weapons. And then outside the movie
I saw blood in the middle of the flower of Queen Anne's lace
and language vanished like a dress come off and the body
vows to remain on earth. I couldn't see through it, but I felt
the fabric of the distance and the threads spun and run through
the warp of the loom materializing something around you.

DEVOTION: *CLOSER*

Fuck off and die, one lover says to the off-screen other
after he gets what he wants: the truth extruded from the lips
and lubricious pink tissue engorged with six quarts of red/white
and factors pumped up on orders of the amygdala. It's Jane Austen
but for the fluids. Inside and dark, we watch the sprocketed stills
run through our measures of identity, our kennings, our damp,
myopic eyes. Inside and dark, the movie's an extravaganza of reds
and yellows, explosive tears, the scrim and fictions move us
into the apology of other lives we can't have ourselves. Stuff blows up.
We know so much. Let me ruin it by telling you that after the accident
and that dilation of the pupils at first sight and the release of dopamine,
he loves her and she him and neither and both others with photographs
and mirrors and the boom mike captures and the tracking shot betrays
as it moves forward the kind of reverse angle doom of the couples.
We look through the window: lovers by a river. We look through
smoke: a nightclub where strangers in makeup and wigs
assume the postures of devotion—prone or bound or like us
inside and dark and the foreground lit as if by the single beam
of a car we are not driving. We know so much.
We know a glance is the romance of the optic nerve
and a blow at an angle so that we keep on going, an oblique
flux that follows impact. On screen the gorgeous face
is like your face, dear heart, I pressed my palms against to still
the fever I could not cool. Nothing was this beautiful and cruel.

DEVOTION: FLIGHT

Woman in the street walking and weeping with purpose in the pale
green organza number that sizzles as she drags her dead mother's
four-wheeled paisley satchel she uses as a carry-on over the bricks
into a cab—a brassy diaphragm and drum muted by the clothes-
stuffed body and the drizzle that's unseasonable with flecks of snow.
A siren in the distance, a paisley of leaves in the streets, the scissoring hush
of the weeping woman's skirt. She's the prima donna of the male slash
female opera that mimics slander or rapture. Luggage a language
of methodical longing like a sonnet, the wound and absence of the other
in a small, cadenced space. She is her belongings. She flies somewhere.
The insides come out, the folds are unfolded, the creases uncreased,
each ruck and pucker expressed. Somewhere the clocks are wrong
by three hours, giving time to the insult or insult to the time no voice
unravels. And there's poetry. Surely there's that syndrome and song.

DEVOTION: ODE

1. TURN

O everyone needs a reason to sing and then an editor, an officer for the crime
and the parole, a rabbi for agreement of number and gender, for singular and plural,
for the prolix and misspelled soul, if we had a soul and not just clouds and a battalion
of neurons firing, firing back at one another. It was what we did as children:
made a war and then another. The rabbi said let it make sense on some level:
the lullaby and the homicide. The rabbi said for every song a shivaree.
And no more home movie and its waaa, and kill the lights, the art, and be neither
a puddle of suffering or a music in the making, and don't step on the singer.

2. COUNTERTURN

Nobody knew how she came to be like that: a parrot speaking her private
Esperanto, like a radio left loudly on in a room, tuned to the Furies, confessing
to a crime she didn't commit (her art), haranguing the government, but in company
she was mute with the silence of a head trauma victim, polite, speaking
in vowels, in yelps, and now I think it was the erotic shyness of being bound
and imprinted by Him, the boss, the sergeant, the head honcho, the dick, her face
a leather mask and words a voodoo that avoided imaginary arrows dipped in poison
making a wound of the lips (genitals of the imagination). She wanted it.
The jaw and cry was magic, was taxing. The sentence was the bliss of the tacit.

3. STAND

And then I heard a voicelike sound and I shouted back
through the polymers and magnets, the cross talk and the hum,
through the lines and beams that were the replicas of nerve.
And we called it phone. And its coils and un were the dendrites and the axons,
Its synapses our gaps. Its membranes were the flat spaces between one,
say, in the East, with a toothless sky, a skyline of battery acid (but the slaves
were freed), and one, say, in the mid-West, water-cured lady of the lakes
where the plane went down with Otis Redding and all my hopes
for Utopia and we called it distance and we breathed into it and cried.

DEVOTION: OCTOBER

Then the crisis call comes in—problems with the heart and the head
and the rest (often), problems with manliness, money, problems
with what love is what with the windfall, what with the wind, October
in the moment you don't know, can't know until *then* the tenderness
from the short fall, the sentiment from the sore, what with your thumb
on a button, your fingers in some danger. *What? Wait. Are you in some
danger?* The voice on the other end says, *but I love him. What?*
I'm listening in the interval that becomes the bardo of wrathful
and peaceful moments with wind. The kid held over the scalding water.
I put the phone down and I was armless, of course, what with the alarm,
what with the harm I could not hear, what with the buzz, what
with the ghosts. The problem was the rest. And the kid already tender,
blue in places, already nibbled on by the soul. Remember the soul?
It's the black, white, sallow, olive, red, black kids I'm afraid for.
Encultured like pearls, although they don't know, can't know until then.
They know wind shears and squalls. They know October shoves you
two-armed into the street where you are tender, and don't know it
in the moment, the brain being scalded by sex and forgetful.
Was that your thumb and forefinger around the nipple? The kids
are a vector for violence living as they do in the wind, and why
should they get roughed up by the articulation of someone's heart
head problem since they have (countable nouns here) spun from straw
as in a fairy tale. The call comes through the corded phone, remember
those? And I'm tethered. And it's unforgiveable. It's later now.
I'm afraid for Raekwon, Ariana, and for the boy named Infinite.

I'm afraid I don't recall the fuckery that was all, that was summer,
spring, fall. The gnats and the midges ghost around the ginkgos,
the city's musk. And swallows sputter in the intervals, the crickets
find the last warm. The (countable noun) is put into a bag to drown.
And you remember the water as warm
and your father as loving and your mother as home.

DEVOTION: AMERIKA

The K we wrote into America was like prying apart the jaws
of the '60s and inserting our heads. The teeth were the '50s—
white, enameled like the fridge. Hanoi was where we were headed,
headless as we were, and fuck Dad eking out his dying. We took the K
from him, Republican golfer that he was, like Ike and his kin.
It was too late to go to Selma or San Francisco, to be clubbed
and dog bitten and loved. Writing it had the dizzying thrill
of self-strangulation or sin. We were never sure if he heard,
upstairs, but fuck him on general principles.
Each accommodating consonant we'd make awkward, hammering
the Ks of the folding chairs with our fists. Apparently he never heard
the manifestos and position papers. Softly, safely, we let the drugs
come over us. We took the K from neocolonial khaki, Yankee,
kike, stroke, bunko artist, the Judas kiss.

DEVOTION: RIMBAUD

To my brother: in his khaki habit like the one the missionaries wore
    who were sent to the windy end of empire to serve and secure,
    he turns in his cubicle, he rends a veil with his pencil,
    he moves a decimal, he breaks and sets code like bone.
        For the poor.

To my brother: in jail in his Wu Wear and absolutes—
    everything's a knife—there's no such thing as silence
    as John Cage said when there was irony and random
    was a tunnel under the symphony of another century.
        For the violated.

To Emma: that demon who was Linnaeus or Levi-Strauss
    in another life, publishing the ideologies and taxonomies of smell—
    fox, rot, scat, gall, goat, and once a rasher of bacon.
        For the cherubim. For the kin.

To the debutant I was: a glistening fly in winter.
        For the fevers of children.

To the man at 60: a turnip disinterred, a peasant in snow with bad shoes.
        For the cult of the exaggerated girl.

To the rich: chattering dolphins in a sea of benzene.
        For the afflicted.

Tonight, in the untowered downtown of Syracuse, the currency
    hardens to the gray slugs the slot machine spits out and as the ghost
    fish smell in the low haphazard heaven, I make this vow to look around.
    For the ones to my right and my left.

DEVOTION: THE GAME

The artist is a creep with his little boxes, but the athlete is a man
who has stolen glory in all its forms, stolen honey in a cup from the gods
and hidden it in his insides where the bees drone. I'm always a boy
as I sit or stand in the shouting place and breathe the doses of men—
smoke and malt—as the night comes down in the exact pattern
of a diamond, a moonlit hothouse of dirt a boy knows is something
to spit on and pat into a shape. Dirt's a cure for the buried someone.
Even as it begins with its anthem, it's lost to me, the exact color
of devotion. So goodbye to the inning and other numbers on scoreboards
and the backs of our team, our blue and red, our lips, our business,
which is to rip into them, a boy learns, or bark at the hit or miss.
Men have skill although I see them fail and fail again and fail to hit
the curve. I'm always a girl as I aww and ooo. What's the infield fly rule?
I tried to watch the grips and tricks, the metaphysics, the spin,
the positions of fast and still, scratch and spit . . . but I thought
in all this infinity, of the Clementes, the Mays, and the Yogis,
of the bats of ash I would have to crack and would I have to squeeze
them home? Would I be asked to sacrifice? Would I belly button it
or break my wrists trying not to swing? There's a box and a zone
in the air and the dirt I must own. To find my way out
or know where it is I sit, I keep my ticket stub in my fist.

DEVOTION: BASEBALL

Pinetar, a sluice of tobacco, sunflower seeds, and juju.
Lena Blackburne rubbing mud, gum, the glues and salves
for doing things fairly—one out of three
swipes at the ball and a flare to right, a dying quail, a 3–
2 change popped up with a *shitfuck*, handcuffed, tomahawked
the high hard stuff or took a backwards K when made to look ugly
as we often were: Humility 3 Arrogance 1 after seven innings. And all
America around us in the sentimental vaudeville. So not the claims
of greened paradise and diamonds and the beauty of the sacrifice
bunt nor the Newtonian symmetries and distances, it was snakes
in the outfield and trances interrupted by a hamstring pull, spit and chew,
geological time spans between ball one and ball two. The meditative silences
likened to prayer were a bus ride where the Latin music blared.
We had a dominant eye. We had a thought, well, not quite a thought,
a thought fouled off in the direction of a woman who could hold a drink,
an oilcan we'd crush like an inside pitch in our dreams. Fast twitch
muscle and jock itch. We scratched our names in dirt.
We wiped our hands on our shirts. As much as we wanted to look good,
we were the bullies of our childhood sliding, cleats up at Juan or Bob
with the fury of the psychopath, Ty Cobb (whose mother
blew his father's head off with a shotgun, so forever playing dead).
I like the silent church before the service begins, Emerson said,
and so too I liked the games no one could see: pepper, shagging flies, b.p.
Got picked off first and waited for a ticket home.
Drafted or matriculated? In a one run game I missed the cut-off man.
Boys my age were dying in Khe Sanh.

DEVOTION: X

X sends a box of photographs packed in Styrofoam: black/whites
of you as a boy in a uniform with a Star of David pinned
to your shoulder, a toothy kid, smiling, but terrified too,
the muscles pulled away from the hole of the mouth and for years
you thought you knew you were glorious marching to the cheers,
carrying a banner that said *Strength through Joy* and another banner
whose words were overexposed in the blaze of the sun. Somebody
must have loved the boy. Somebody ransomed him, hid him
in the middle class, rubbed butter on his lips, handed him a banner
of happiness that flapped in the wind made clement for him,
the boy given mathematics and music, a tempo, an allegro
that quickened him and forbade lingering, forbade dream,
forbade remembering. Somebody bourgeoised the boy, the dark closets
abolished for the brightest rooms where there was shit and the snow
was Styrofoam. There was a memory of something in the corners
of his eyes when he awoke, sleep, she called it, the mother
who had chosen him, *go back to sleep, go back to sleep*, there is
nothing to be afraid of, and thus the particular could not linger,
and he could not see anything but the sun. But who was X?
Who were you? And who was this Bruce Smith, the lightweight boxer,
Bruce Smith, the singer of the blues, the siren's zero, bomber
of pure order? And what were the zeros, ones, and twos,
and the hunger and the words on the banner? What was the aperture?
And what was the existing light? What was the saturation and hue?

DEVOTION: INFANT JOY

Faces have clocks? Not so fast you tall, loud breathing places.
What's with the holes in yours, liars, agitators? Airplanes
you say, but I don't believe you after 9/11. Clap yourself
out of whack and something at the end of you adagios
and away. Near sky. How far? Come down. What now?
I see fly wow into you and out wow. Phht. Baa. Feed me
or drop me as you do down, you operators, but let me
dog it in the dust you left me. What gorgeous. What No?
Where was the sky when I hit my head? Ow. Don't even try
to console me you bulldozers, you Zambonis. What *does* the sheep say?
Try to keep up. Faces go away. That's funny? It's yuck or No.
Don't do the terror thing with holes. Don't you heartbeats know
about object permanence? I'll go down but not before you arm
and name me. Bunny is funny. You too. It's about time?

DEVOTION: INFANT SORROW

ABC me to sleep. Brain me. Nacht me through it all, the bit
of the Bush administration. Safe as the baby in the tree
top, bough breaks, kick, kick, kick. I'm a romantic with hands
no different from it, her, them. I am my dirt, my baby spilt.
Basta with your pronouns, the peek-a-boo hums and errs.
Give me nouns, no tricks, orphan swim in, kick, kick,
fin and spit. You masses, you hisses, I am not your diction.
Thrill me with sugar, more sugar, you sacs and humps. We
(baby, puffs, sticks) are outbreaks of republicans and ghosts—
gas, laughs, more sugar please you bigger things, more sheet.
I (you, them, downy him) am not your style, you wanted one
and you gots. I eat all the difficult patriarchal stuff and shit.
Sleep me past the washed, rocked, bashed (kick). What's fin
and fowl. I want to be like Dickinson. I'm going underground.

DEVOTION: THE REPUBLIC

Now that baby Claire is here in a pink hat and any number
of functioning fingers and toes and a face like a German philosopher,
it's time to turn to the strictures of art and to resurrect the habeas corpus
laws—we'd be ashamed if Claire had to spend one minute more
here terrified by our time, our slim evidence, our duration.
It's time to crawl back into the womb of the republic. The adjustors
of air, the speculators kicked us out for inciting feelings of desire
and pleasure, alien feelings, bad behaviors, sucking, crying,
and pissing on their parade. It's time to return to the particulars
of the valves—heart and horn—for how else will we make a music
for her? And to the immensities of nerve and to the record
of when we found ourselves *more truly and more strange*—the end
of a poetry that cries against Cheney who is strangely somebody
with a heart as baby Claire is truly somebody with a heart only cuter
in her pink hat and closer to feeling mothered, that particular immensity
that records the body of evidence of what it felt like to be delivered
into and from the glorious, unnamed harm of America. Claire,
your mother will explain this to you later: the threat, the speculations
and productions of your time, Dick Cheney and Kirkuk
and Tikrit, which sound like the scat you make lying down
to sleep. How can we look at the smirk on your face
and the ten toes and not think about another way of thinking?
So I helped with the late night feeding, and when Claire was asleep,
I went to sleep and dreamed in a shameless way that I had breakfast
with the V.P., milk and sweet rolls, and I listened to him and
he listened to me, our remorse was great, our remorse was a trumpet,
as I listened to him and we forgave each other
not that it was ours to forgive.

DEVOTION: ACTIVE SHOOTER PROTOCOL

Policy was to circumvent the building. Policy was.
But by the time we did that everyone inside was dead
and we were shooting at ourselves. Our armored heads. Our hearts
in vests. I blame architecture. I blame our open arms and our
forefathers. What was that angsty music the boy was listening to?
I loved the plot that held us and my distorted voice, but since then
there's been ten years of television, so I'm telling you
don't stop for the child, even if the child holds another child.
Don't stop to resolve the questions of the kingdom of heaven
or the cracks and fissures in all your talk. (You, who cowrote
the memo.) No time for arias in the secured area
which is what the elementary, vocational, arts magnet, junior high
school is now, locked down, and just yesterday it was dance
and African drumming and poetry with Ms. G, who called it
the center of consciousness for the friable universe. The rescue
is no rope and no ransom. We make a diamond, first one, then two,
then one. It moves forward as it ignores the hall made slippery
with blood. The music that boy listened to made between his ears
a horror. I blame the art. I blame the law. We're all the deputies
of his dream. Don't stop even if you see your face flash back
in a window or papers that lift and fall like failed wings from the walls.
Don't stop for the child that calls or asks a question. Walk past
the songbirds and the sighs and dioramas and the halos and the clouds
and the trophies of the jocks. The rescue completely falls apart
when you try to do smart. You with your credentials.
You with your salvation stories. Your purchases. Your blunt
trauma pads to make a better place for our loneliness.

DEVOTION: CAR WRECK

After the wreck, I found myself leaking
the blue/green fluids of the sea, like Icarus, speaking

to anyone who would listen about the stall
and spin into the hard, brilliant surface, spirals

of fire and a new tongue sewed up with stitches,
but I lived. I had to learn to relinquish

what the tongue did or unlearn, unhold
the world and my face a blindfold

to beauty. So my life
as assassin/midwife

was done. I put down the babies
in their basinets and the bodies

in their mannerist beds, I'd mop up.
I let go of the wrist with its dull thud

as the smithereens worked their way out
of me, little bloody slivers of the devout.

DEVOTION: NATURE

I liked it, but not so close to me—clouds, sure, the nimbocumulus, yes,
but not the low pressures and slow cyclones of the sky fallen
into the mouth you whispered, you lied, you apologized with.
The panoramas, the calendar shots, the scenic overlooks I pulled over
and awed and overlooked. Nature was a bright lamp and a big book
written in Urdu I tried to read until I fell asleep (and then
the bedbugs rose before dawn to make their aubade from my blood).
Nature was a booted wander in the Lake District where some saw
the sublime and some saw the ego (like the inside of the eye—
the red hue and the blind spot where the nerve leaves its orbit
for the lie and apology of the mind). The beautiful, tragic boys
were made dizzy by ravines, by all sensation. Nature spoke to them
through many storms and atmospheres, thrushes, clear universes,
murky puddles. It spoke for them, *in scorn of mortal power*. (Shelly,
on Mont Blanc.) I saw a rivulet and the devout, enthusiastic grasses
when I left the borough and then California and then the Ganges,
but the lynchings of the ghosts in my Mesopotamia had made it
taxidermy for me: a corpse with purple lips, grotesque and sexy.
My people painted it or scraped the paint off to give it that natural
look. We dipped the blossom in batter and fried and ate it.
We were the infinite apes at infinite keyboards typing it,
letting it in or keeping it out. I liked the pollination and slow mo
photos of the seed to leaf, but not the dark forests, the isotopes,
certain germs at work, and the sea that buoyed you up
then took you down. I liked it when it was food or Jerusalem. Now
the clouds are ripped and the likenesses are skewed. It's warm.
And where are you? And the bees. And the ice floes for our feelings.

DEVOTION: THE INSECTS

The dazzling displays or the sham shadows, the ones born
in 1926 in America, white-shirted elegant, work-shirted diffident,
who were prophetic or perfect or sad, flaneurs or frotteurs, workers
who survived the bomb and the imagining, mouths swabbed with acids,
the swarm of men who did not conceive of us, who did not want us,
although we jarred them, gassed them, found them inside our books
like silverfish with ancient bodies and small black eyes. We found them
near the drip, near the flame, in the bodies of question marks and coppers.
We found them in our chests and heads, in our suitcases, in our backyards,
closets, and luscious cul de sacs. We found them and killed them,
but they could not be killed. They were the dark matter of the fat planet,
unseen (for the most part) but supranumerous (because we forget),
these pests and pollinators, these bodies of memory (these bodies are
memory), so many nymphs and midges, scales and mealy bugs,
dark particles unseen but known by their gravitas, their bathos,
their itch, their twitching antennae—clubbed or bristled—their sobbing,
sucking mouthparts, their 50,000 eyes. We blinked and missed the naiads,
the smoky winged things, particles of energy and distance (rips, snarls),
opposite charges to the forces of the vast American prevalence,
singing to annihilate the giant. They were Napoleons loving the god
that loved battalions, lousy with number. Born in the evening,
dead by dawn, but what a song: an inconsolable male chorus,
a cloud singing their cante jondo for the female, as they did in 1926
in America, seizing her and falling to the riverbank with her
where they wrote the poetry of this life: dung hills and rays of daylight

they tasted and touched with their antennae as they pushed, like beetles,
the sun across the sky and became the name for what came into being,
this brilliant nothing against the great something, jewels for the heart
weighed in the next life against the feather of truth. They wrote
in elfin and blue. What they said was in form and flinging.
Heart: do not testify against me in the presence of the Lord of Things.

DEVOTION: DUSK

A copy of a copy of a copy
of a rumor of glory.
                    Sacrifice this,
I said to my god with my indoor voice, my sloppy
ding an sich, my interior with extension cord and abyss.

Night is either everything else or etcetera,
I can't tell which. I'm afraid of the phenomenon
you bring back from sleep: the unfurled viscera
of the kittens, the street fight with Frantz Fanon.

You can't pretend you don't love the world
in translation
                    although day is a literal place
with 80-some pregnant high school girls, god
did not father from the looks of the erasures
of their faces. We will have to kill the kids
with golden shovels, their mouths like orchids.

DEVOTION: RACE TRAITOR

Now the breath of Charlie Parker through the sax—the rapid,
passing beauty minus the blackness and the smack—is all our breath.
And Malcolm Little, indicter of devils, bandit, reefer man, pimp,
and not-yet prophet is our master X. And the voice of the "wonder
boy preacher," Solomon Burke of Philadelphia, died out
as my childhood in Philadelphia died out only to materialize
in a gospel choir from the South where I heard the paramour
of my interior shout, "Take Me, Shake Me," minus the burden
and the Lord. These men and the Browns: Jim and James, made my skin
itch and I scratched and watched them on TV where they were beamed
to me in small, mutant grayscale flames—white the coolest,
black the most devout—that flickered before me, (took me, shook me),
mothered me, these men, their faces the first moving thing I saw
from my crib. I fixed them like a baby to a face drawn on a washcloth
wrapped around a clock. Mother time, father milk. I tocked
to the insistent tick I heard in rock or the knocked-back blues
or that strange listening to the skin and the pigments of the nerves
the saxophonists did. I resisted the men I was given: papas, nadas,
jurors, the potentate of this, the secretary of that, my white ideology,
which was vaguely a belief, vaguely a machine that worked for me,
smokeless, well riveted, given to entropy and sadness and William James
and all the lumas of much too much experience. White worked in pure
utilitarian ways that were oiled and greased by the gods, the very gods
the strange new powers talked me out of. And suddenly I'm barking
the obscure, excited yelps of sex and other suffering and the unforeseen
consequence of being not black, not red, not tinted much on the grayscale,
not all that happy, agitated enough to cause a crack in the deeded country
and the interior nation and I would do nothing for my skin
but shed, and the dust is what James Brown returned to

but beautifully with sequins and screams and Bird flew above
or Jim Brown kicked up and all the would-be tacklers ate,
dust that X spat on, breathed on, and shaped the mud
into a man and Solomon Burke from his throne sang and I sang
along in private, because I could not join but I could not remain
the same, and the singing was refusing subtly, subtly refusing.

DEVOTION: FUTURISMO

We cared less about the things and more about the smears and blurs
and fluxing stuff. We hated the depiction of history and yesterday's
devotions. We put on goggles and sped past God and the seductive
punctures in the skin of his son. We put wings on everything—
glued feathers to our ankles, flew, if you closed your eyes
and thought of beauty as an ungainly filly that cantered and nickered
as it stood still. We entered the future backwards, not aliens, not robots,
more like workers with dispensable shovels rising into the blasted
new/old country, becoming the bosses of ourselves, firing ourselves,
grumbling about the work. We confused beauty with velocity,
airplanes with auras, because what's a moving object but a breed
of being spread across the retina, numina, reds and yellows,
the present ripped and difficult and everything's a space ship.
And what about the future of the soft machine? Señor gets tired.
Señor leaks from his gaskets, needs new bearings and shocks,
beauty is killing him. Señor stays awake all night as the wind
throws its language against the window like a blind bird body.
A kiss should be like this. In the morning the sticky, catalytic smell
of hot patch and pleas for mercy. The flights of pigeons, the entrails
of road kill mean my country will suffer and murmur and shit
and go blind. The beautiful obliterating snows will drift and melt
and freeze and ravish the surface and light will glaze the trash—
the most meager skin made magnificent. Beauty's neither
here nor there but deadly and Señor's ashes still not scattered
but carried twice to new cities, X-rayed and checked through airports.
"Organs?" "No, ashes." The formal feeling works backwards
from letting go to stupor to great pain. Señor wants a future,

wants a smear of violence or color, wants a beholder
to see him like a tulip bulb sunk with bone meal and wintered
and unfurled come spring like a picture of the floating world.
Señor, on what things will we stick our kisses? I think
halfway between a wheelbarrow of dirt and a facsimile machine,
is beauty. I think it's a horse that moves between the skin and the unseen.

DEVOTION: SUN

South of Cincinnati: a lot of scorched that (a lot of this) lost
in the Not-I incised by six lanes (lane from a British schoolboy
hymn) that we call August or science or home.
Near becomes foreclosed and far becomes a Doppler
of the beloved and still lives at 75 with radio Jesus everywhere
on the air (like a test of the Emergency Broadcast System).
A face comes out of the clouds, a lake of fire ahead like science,
Jesus, Home Depot, and the over voice like a mobbed-up
Sinatra, appealing to your sense of power (+less), your sense
of Scotch and Soda. Then the sun burns a hole in the film
and makes an even greater sun that halos the round bales
in the fields and pours through the hole a molten gold
around your head like one of Giotto's sobbing angels.
You begin to see the way the bodiless mob controls
the material as the wind is a gold you move through, chest deep,
as in the aftermath of storm. You're dead, Sinatra says, unless
(−un) you're one of the cool elected to move horizontal, but
not moving at all (seated, driving, bored), your pulse a diesel.
A hawk rides the thermals. You slay another dragonfly
on the windshield. You're complicit with Mobil. The radio says,
you're never entering the kingdom of heaven—a shady lane
with butterflies—while you enter the endless red generalization
of the middle you take an aspirin for. Tar bars beat out a rumba
(Cuba, Africa) that sings failure or future, rapture or vulture,
who can tell? When Huck and Jim dropped below Cairo,
more orphan and slave than before, more beloved of each other
(more cruel) than before, they moved through the hoax
and scorched that and the whiskey of the middle

into the (loveless, ruthless) American. Now you're a pin
dropped on a map moved by your mind (heated like Egypt).
It's not all matter. It's a butter that's god and other, squinting
distance, no nearer nor farther, south of Cincinnati the world
(minus New York and Vegas) is female as much as we try to truck it
(cargo, capture). The light is gasoline poured over everything.

DEVOTION: MIDRASH

Strings did things to you: held you at one end while you
became deranged, made you forget the inamour, swerved
around the realpolitik, the stink, made a cup for the god
thirst, hid the tent city, relieved the money grief for three bars,
four, bandaged the open sore, realized and blamed the systems
for a blink or two, made (poem) the consternation of coins
falling through the slot on the coffer of the bus (chromatics
and discords) seem like the truth of the end of suffering
(the third noble truth). They took things far. Strings made
wings of things (nouns verbs), held down Gulliver, made
flavors and spins of our duration, made the guitar
a question mark, lost the thread. They made the rain
come down for a couple of beats, which was the riches,
the tender, the fat stacks, the math. So the poem (the great film
festival of spirits and sobs) goes on with its fornicating ways
and its clemency for the engines (little, think, could)
which keep it suffering (the first noble truth). The audience
for this (we can't agree) will be you or homies, Buddhists,
Prince Hal in Birkenstocks, birds, texting men, enraptured,
ruptured girls left alone in the tent city where they summon
their darlings through perplexed strings. How do you know
the levels of our sadness without a string across an opening?
How do you get a flood in a bowl, a core sample of the unsung
summoned from pluck (you), the synthetics or cat gut
of zero sum? Strings made you midrash the stuff, sniff
out the perfume (the ocean, the flower), chew the root, express
the part where we're talking to ourselves from the part
that's not. We have a way (fourth truth) we employ

against the day depending on whether you're Keats
with your nose pressed against the window of the sweet
shop (devotion, attachment—the second noble truth)
or whether you're the woman on the bus—
two kids, one crying, eating a cracker from the floor,
one about to cry from the what for.

DEVOTION: CROWS

At the end of the song, a sadness, a sexual sadness: and you forgot
you were in a song, as good songs make you do when they cover up
your overheated body in a cape and you shrug it off and come back
to sing again because you forgot the song doesn't end like you forgot
the century goes on: remember the barking dogs and ice floes
and funny clothes of last century and the centuries before
the ones with art and the middle passage, holocaust and denial,
talking in our cells of food we didn't get, and the plantation
of her skin where I was a slave trying to work for my freedom.
I worked for a hundred years in the fields from can't see to
can't see although it was only three winters measured
in the gratuitous music of my twitching, sleepless love
and the murders of crows in the lower air of the city at dusk
like badly thrown, badly drawn stars liquidating an existence.
The crows speak of the rape, the tongue cut out, the children killed
and baked into a pie, with the one word they have. They speak of
my love. They speak of James Brown, with their one word, *aw*.
The crows know what he meant when he went from 2/4 to 1/3
on the downbeat. The crows know odd and otherworldly.
They know syncopation and change; they've been in the wind.
They know the fame of the flames. The crows know South Carolina
and Augusta, Georgia, the slave block and the cotton fields
and corn fields unseeded by will and the scarecrows and the handguns.
They've eaten fast food and they've eaten roadkill. They've been
to the Apollo with their one syllable. They know the exigency and ecstasy
and speak it. They tell of the breaking and entering and the shoeshine,

the scuffed surface buffed and rebuffed with a rag snap, until it's a glossy
blackness: from degrade comes jubilee comes the glad things on 1 and 3
the color of their wings. They have taken us to the bridge.
They have used tools and none greater than the drum.
By their one word they have abducted us and sit
in the crotch of the trees rasping and jittering.

DEVOTION: ROMAN

In dream the mother says, Go outside until I (die, fix dinner). Go on,
get out (horizon, hazy nature). There are multiple takes. She says,
Get (beg, breed, bag), Get (buy into, sicken). There are always apertures
and exits, pinhole visions. *It is always something else in the end*, the artist said
about his subject matter (drift, swerve). And I go out into the hot alley
of concrete and tar we lived in after the war (there are multiple wars)
a matrix of lime and mortar and stone (mostly space, mostly thrown),
honeysuckle and nightshade on fences, the late model cars of the (20th,
21st) century, illuminated by water from hoses, suds from buckets poured
over them, copper and steel blue, scarabs (Fords, Studebakers), products
of our rags. They will Los Angeles and Alabama us (low and freedom
riders). They will chop and channel us (my manifold, my medium).
In dream I go out into the frontier where TV rifles ricocheted.
There are many wars. I go out into the village where I am the prodigy
of chalk on sidewalk before rain (love song, noir). In steel blue shadow
or copper sun, at the edge of shallow pools from the scourings, I paint
my tromp l'oeil making the concrete concrete. I go out (body, sigh)
into a greeny backyard plot (my end, my dandelion) crossed overhead
with wires like the grid of perspective (god, art). It's dark when I go out,
in dream, into steamy July, and get realized. I go out and I'm a Roman
changed by the sight of all the crucifixions on the boulevard,
or not, looking away, casting my lot with my friends for the dead
man's clothes. I go out and meet someone who no longer is.
I go out and witness boys with sticks break apart a hive like a piñata
and enter the purgatory (Pompeii, Philadelphia) of shame (me, I was
the boy). I go out into Seattle where I join the line for the shelter

even though I am in love. I go out and the scale shifts. In one
of the manifold exits (pleasure, pressure) I go out into cloud
that takes the impression of my face (fugitive, felon) and keeps it
as evidence. Many hues, many masks. I go out into Syracuse
(my Berlin, my opium) and invent the kiss I will give you. I forget
the begetter. I try to charm (spell, sing) my way back in.

DEVOTION: THE UNBIDDEN

Then the Fuckheads come with their memes and dreams of another
time. They come like rats in a fairy tale with pipes and hats (and fevers
and fleas). They're Zoloft calm. They're wind in a canyon.
And you feel a cool, don't you?, you feel a childhood fall.
The Fuckheads smell like ether (or glue). Their faces
milk-carton familiar and horrible. Terrible is what they are.
They want to save you. They want to slap you silly. They pet
the kitty. They bring gossip, glossies, kisses, the Billboard
Top Ten. They've got questions for further study. Now, a loud
chorus of Aida, now a prolonged motorcycle growl. They recite,
in unison, the Tao. They've got their credentials, their possessive
pronouns. They've had tea with the mullah, haven't you?
They finger your quills. They shake your snow globe until all
New York shivers. They've been weaned too early, these strange
angels, and are angry and look everywhere for milk—in your junk
drawer, in your sheets, and in the stashes of music you don't want
them in: your Smokey Robinson, your Muddy Waters. The Fuckheads
want your firstborn son. They'll spin your straw like Rumpelstiltskin,
touch your necklace, your ring, your tongue. They're looking for
your Lucifer. They're looking for your sugar. They seek out things
to gnaw because that's what rodent angels do. They look long
at your skull. They lick. They purr. They bring the talking cure
although they carry daggers. They want to know the story
of your story, not just what happened but what gives
and what are you after? Are you famous? Are you a mannish boy
in a mohair suit? They came without the blinding visions,
the secrets, the money, left without exchanging information
as if what you have are innocent intentions.
You wait and in that time you don't kill.

DEVOTION: FLY

A fly like an envoy for the Lost Boys or a delegate sent to dicker with the dead.
Buzz wants out or in? Does it descend from one who grazed the face
of Dickinson and whispered in her ear the middle octave key of F?
Does it want nectar or the dead, and which am I? Vectors for fugue
and spontaneous bruising. Vectors for pestilence and gods who call
for sacrifice. Shit seraph, heaven worm, world eye, scholar bent over
the heated pages of the Coptic translating the words *matter* and *heaven*
in its three-week paradiso. Fly worries everything. Fly walks on the ceiling.
Fly works its rosary, a discalced nun of doubt, our intercessionary,
while we are free to be evermore certain about our God and the war.
Fly buzzes in the blown-open pages of the tiny novellas everyone carries
scattered like dreams in which we were all the characters. Fly already at it,
its story, a secondhand story, before smoke and a steel-blue wash
over everything. Looking up the way the myrmidons looked up
at the sun, skeptical, sweaty while they killed the ram and ewe,
strung the bow, lifted timbers. It was their job to fight
for someone's love and rage, someone's beauty worth dying for.